# Can I tell you about Tourette Syndrome?

*Can I tell you about...?*

The "Can I tell you about...?" series offers simple introductions to a range of limiting conditions. Friendly characters invite readers to learn about their experiences of living with a particular condition and how they would like to be helped and supported. These books serve as excellent starting points for family and classroom discussions.

*Other subjects covered in the "Can I tell you about...?" series*

**ADHD**

**Adoption**

**Asperger Syndrome**

**Asthma**

**Dementia**

**Dyslexia**

**Epilepsy**

**OCD**

**Parkinson's Disease**

**Selective Mutism**

**Stuttering/Stammering**

# Can I tell you about Tourette Syndrome?

A guide for friends, family and professionals

MAL LEICESTER
Foreword by Julie Collier
Illustrated by Apsley

Jessica Kingsley *Publishers*
London and Philadelphia

First published in 2014
by Jessica Kingsley Publishers
73 Collier Street
London N1 9BE, UK
and
400 Market Street, Suite 400
Philadelphia, PA 19106, USA

*www.jkp.com*

**Library of Congress Cataloging in Publication Data**
Leicester, Mal, author.
Can I tell you about Tourette syndrome? : a guide for
friends, family and professionals / Mal Leicester ;
foreword by Julie Collier ; illustrated by Apsley.
pages cm
ISBN 978-1-84905-407-2 (alk. paper)
1. Tourette syndrome--Juvenile literature. I. Apsley, illustrator. II. Title.
RC375.L45 2014
616.8'3--dc23
2013030784

**British Library Cataloguing in Publication Data**
A CIP catalogue record for this book is available from the British Library

ISBN 978 1 84905 407 2
eISBN 978 0 85700 806 0

Printed and bound in Great Britain

To my grandson, Aidan David Dover, with love.

# Contents

# Foreword

I first met Mal Leicester at one of our Support Group meetings. She had contacted Tourettes Action looking for family support in her area and kindly volunteered to coordinate a new TA support group.

I was so excited when Mal mentioned that she was writing this book about Tourette Syndrome (TS), and I knew that with her extensive background in education and disability, together with her personal family experience of TS, it would make her the ideal author and I couldn't wait to read it!

I had a message today, from a mum I met at a recent meeting. She thanked me for organising the meeting and said how wonderful it had been to meet other parents in the same situation. She had tried to talk to her son about his tics, but found it very difficult to hold his attention. This book will be ideal for parents and children to sit and read together and for the whole family to explore life with TS. Children will relate to Max's story and adults will gain more information and insight into this condition. I know it will help so many similar families in the future.

TS has such a stigma attached to it and even now, in the 21st century, it is misunderstood by many. Some see it as the swearing disorder and someone once asked me if it was a real condition! We have such a long way to go with raising awareness and this book is another big step in the right direction.

I have had the great pleasure of meeting lots of people of all ages with TS, most of whom are talented, intelligent and creative people, who want to be accepted for who they are as individuals and for others to see past their tics.

I would like to see a copy of this book in the library of every school in the UK. It will help teachers to gain a greater understanding and Max's story would be ideal for peer group awareness in schools.

It's up to all of us to help raise awareness, to break down the barriers and to reduce the stigma, so that people living with TS can lead their life to the full, without feeling isolated and let down by our society.

*Julie Collier*
*Groups Manager*
*Tourettes Action*

# Acknowledgements

I wish to thank Sarah Tanner for the efficient preparation of the manuscript, Lucy Buckroyd for her advice and encouragement and Tony Phillips-Smith (Apsley) for his super illustrations. For helpful comments I am also indebted to Julie Collier, Suzanne Dobson, Jane Fowlie, Joe Kilgariff and Roger Twelvetrees.

# Introduction

This book has been written to help children, parents and teachers to understand Tourette Syndrome better.

- It is a child friendly book to share with children who have TS. They can talk about how it affects them and understand that there are many other children with TS too. They are not alone. It is also intended to help the children to understand that tics are not something that they are doing wrong. It is not their fault.

- Children and young people who do not have TS can read about the difficulties faced by a child who does. It will tell them what TS is and how they can help. With better understanding they will be less worried by tics and more ready to be friendly and kind.

- And of course parents, teachers and other professionals can learn more about TS too and be more able to support children with TS. For these concerned adults there are tips about such support, additional information and suggestions for recommended reading at the end.

By taking the child's point of view, this book humanises children with a condition that can present challenging behaviours and it helps us to understand how the children themselves experience the world and what it feels like to experience unremitting, involuntary tics.

This particular book is greatly needed because most people, including most teachers, do not know much about TS. Indeed many people think it means swearing a great deal when in fact only 10 per cent of people with TS suffer from involuntary swearing (coprolalia). It is important that everyone develops more understanding of the condition. Even though only 1 per cent of children have it, any parent may have such a child and any teacher at some point may eventually have a child with TS in their class. It is crucial to the well-being and educational development of such children that their parents, other children and teachers all understand this syndrome and react appropriately to the tics and behaviours associated with it. The sections that follow aim to encourage a sympathetic understanding and also to provide practical advice.

"I have Tourette Syndrome and this book will tell you about it."

"You can't tell straight away that I have Tourette Syndrome. I look like most other boys. But you might notice that I blink a lot or screw up my eyes or blow on my hands. Sometimes I nod my head or hunch my shoulders. I also do a growl noise in my throat or do whistles. These are called tics. I don't want to do them, but I can't help it.

Having TS means I am really good at some things, but I find some other things hard. I am so good at concentrating on things I like doing, such as drumming and karting, my brain can forget to make me tic. Even though I know my TS is always there, it's great to have a rest from my tics because usually I can't stop them unless I make a great effort to hold them back. Even then they will have to come out after a while. It's like playing at not blinking with your friend. You both have to blink in the end.

But having TS means I find it hard to concentrate on things I'm not interested in. Sometimes at school, when my tics are jerking me about, it's like they use up all my concentration and all my energy.

It is very frustrating to find my body making jerks and my voice making noises which I don't want to make. Sometimes the frustration builds up until I feel really angry."

"Nurse Joe at the Tourette Syndrome clinic told me that people with TS like to learn by doing things and it's true. I like to drive a kart or play computer games. I get bored at school when we do sitting down things for too long like reading and writing. Nurse Joe also said TS people are often musical. I like music and I am learning to play the guitar and the drums.

Another thing that Nurse Joe told me is that people with TS are usually empathetic. This means we are understanding when other people feel sad. For instance, I like to help my mum because she can't walk very well. And one day at school a tic made me wipe my own face when I saw a tear run down another boy's cheek! I felt sorry for him and wanted him to feel better. My throat clearing tic can get triggered when someone else has a frog in their throat. Once a boy thought I was making fun of him so he got angry and told me to stop. Later when he understood about TS he said he was sorry."

"Sometimes other children ask me why I do my tics which just come for no reason and sometimes change to different ones."

"Sometimes people ask me what Tourette Syndrome is. It means having tics which you can't control or help doing. TS always gives people movement tics (called motor tics) and noise tics (called vocal tics), but not always the same ones.

Mum and Dad first noticed my tics when I was five. I began to blink my eyes a lot and to make a growl noise. Since then I have had some new motor tics: head nodding, shoulder hunching, and some which you can't see me doing like clenching my tummy, curling my toes. I also have had some new vocal tics: sniffing, throat clearing, barking. I sometimes get teased at school because of this, which only makes my tics worse.

Some tics are called compulsive tics which means you feel an urge to do something such as touch things a certain number of times. It's a bit like having an urge to scratch an itch. Sometimes I have to scratch my leg about five times and then do the same on the other leg or I have to pretend I'm a dog and do a bark. This even seems weird to me!

Many children lose their tics when they become adults. I hope I lose mine too!"

"It is great when people
accept me as I am."

"When I started school no one would play with me because they thought my tics were strange. This made me sad and I longed to join in.

My teacher made a boy called Dylan my "buddy"[1] and now we are good friends. My mum and dad have helped me make friends by letting me do hobbies like karting. My dad even helped out at Beavers so I was not worried about going. After this I was happy to go to Cubs on my own.

After the teacher talked to my parents and me about it, we also had a lesson on Tourette Syndrome that helped my class understand what it is. The children were much kinder afterwards and wanted to know how they could help me.

Some children in my class are so used to my tics that they don't even notice them much any more.

I always feel nervous meeting new children because I worry they will notice my tics and think that I am weird. It really helps me when children are friendly and just accept me as I am.

I wish people would see *me* more than they see my tics!"

---

1 A buddy system can be arranged by a school to help promote friendship and support between peers. Sensitive, friendly and mature students can be selected to partner with others and spend time with them in break times.

"It's awesome to have hobbies, like karting, drumming, computer games and cooking, that you love so much you stop ticcing."

"Mum and Dad know that my tics get less when I relax and help me with this by stroking my hair. Being active and using up some energy also helps so they take me out on my bike or play football with me.

I like to go to new places with someone I know, otherwise I can get worried and my tics can get worse.

I love playing with other children and having them over to my house to play. I've made some great friends from my hobbies too.

Mum and Dad don't try to make me stop ticcing which I can't do anyway. They don't make me feel bad about it.

We don't talk about Tourette Syndrome much at home but I know I can talk to Mum and Dad about it if I want to. They don't talk about my TS to other people in front of me, but I'm happy for them to let some people like my teachers and other parents know about it.

They gave my teacher a leaflet from Tourettes Action and this helped her to understand even more. My parents and school are both on the same side – my side."

"It really helps when teachers try
to understand what it is like to
have Tourette Syndrome!"

"Tourette Syndrome can make some lessons hard. For example:

- I find it hard to concentrate when tics use up my energy and attention.

- When my eyes, head or neck tic I find it hard to read.

- When my eyes, hands and arms tic, it stops me writing neatly.

- Vocal tics can interfere with reading aloud.

- My leg or arm sometimes jerks and stops me catching, throwing or kicking a ball properly.

It's important my teachers understand about TS. One day my usual teacher was ill and we had a cover teacher who didn't know me. I did growl tics when all the children were sitting on the carpet for a story and she thought I did this on purpose. I was sent out of the class for being naughty. This made me feel very angry and misunderstood."

"I really love my fidget toy."

"When no one ever chose me for their partner and their team I felt bad, as though there was something wrong with me. It felt as if people would never like me. That made my tics worse.

My teacher noticed this and did some lessons about making friends. Everyone learned more about how to be friendly. You have to be nice to each other and to take turns. I always used to want to choose the rules of the games because then I didn't have to concentrate on learning what they were. I know now that I have to take turns and do my best to concentrate when someone else makes up the rules.

I also have a link teacher who links up with me every week to make sure that I'm not having any problems. She is really nice. She even watches out for me at playtimes. Best of all, she gave me a small rubber monkey as a 'fidget object'. She said my hands could play with it while I was listening to her talking or reading to us. The fidget toy helps me to feel calm and relaxed."

"When the doctor told us about my Tourette Syndrome we didn't know much about it and wanted to know more. Now we have our Tourettes Action group and the doctors at the clinic to help us."

"Children are born with Tourette Syndrome but their parents don't usually find out until they are older. I was about five but my friend and his mum and dad didn't know until he was ten. Some people think your tics are just bad habits you have grown into. In a way it is good to find out that these tics are TS and not something you should be able to stop doing.

My doctor was very kind and explained that it wasn't my fault that I had TS. He told me about support groups like Tourettes Action and sent me to see some special doctors at the medical centre. I met Nurse Joe who was friendly and told us all about TS.

Nurse Joe got me to say where I thought I was on the TS scale. I had to work out how much TS interferes with my life and everything I want to do. Mum, Dad, Nurse Joe and I all agreed – I was moderate, which is about halfway between mild and severe.

Someone who has mild TS may not even know because they may think the tics are just habits and not notice them after a while. But someone who has severe TS has more to cope with than me."

"Our support group meets once every month at fun places and sometimes in a Children's Centre which has lots of toys."

"It turned out that there was no support group where we live so we set one up. Tourettes Action helped all the families to meet. We were all very happy about this and I met some great friends. Mum and Dad were very pleased to be able to meet and talk to other parents.

Since then we have all been to an adventure playground and we've been to other places and enjoyed ourselves.

When we are together for some reason we sometimes tic more but we all really like being able to hang out with other kids who know what it is like to have Tourette Syndrome.

Most of the children who go to my Tourettes Action group have more than TS. Two of the group have TS and Asperger syndrome; one of them has TS and ADHD (which is short for attention deficit hyperactivity disorder); and one of them has TS, autism and ADHD.

If you have two problems they may make each other worse. You may need extra help at school."

"I like machines. It was awesome to see a picture of my own brain."

"The doctor says that my Tourette Syndrome is because of a problem in the bits of my brain that control movements. Sometimes a tic just comes and sometimes I know it will come because I get a tickly, itchy feeling just before the tic happens. The tic happens and sends the itchy feeling away.

There is a lot no one knows yet about how the brain works and how we can stop it going wrong and there are people doing research on this to find out more. I recently had an MRI scan and got to keep a picture of my brain!

Some people think that stress causes tics but this isn't quite right. The brain causes TS, but for lots of people stress can trigger the brain into making tics happen more whereas relaxation can help reduce tics.

Dad says he thinks I tic more when I'm tired. I don't think he's just saying this to get me into bed early! I do feel better when I am wide awake.

Medication helps some people with severe tics to have them less. I don't need to take any, but if my tics get worse then I could try it.

When I'm a few years older I may be able to have some help with learning how to have a bit more control of my tics. You can turn them into other movements which people don't notice so much. This is called habit reversal training. I would like to learn to be the boss of my own brain!"

"My dog Goldie is my best friend."

"These are some of the things that help me. I love stroking my dog. It makes me feel quiet and peaceful. I wish all children with Tourette Syndrome could have a dog or a cat or a rabbit to stroke!

My mum and dad cut the labels out of the back of my new jumpers or T shirts. Scratchy clothes feel itchy and make my shoulder and neck tics worse.

Good friends really help me. Once when some children called me names my friend Dylan stood up for me. It felt great to have such a good friend.

As well as the hobbies I told you about, I also find swimming, singing and playing games send my tics away, but if it is a game I don't understand or find difficult I get worried and my tics can come on more.

Mum says we are all good at something and no one is good at everything. We all need to find our own things that we are good at and that we enjoy doing."

"My birthday party was at the karting
place and I drove the fastest lap.
It made me feel really good."

"This is my list of do's and don'ts if you have Tourette Syndrome.

## Do's

- Try out different hobbies to find some that may help you to escape from your tics for a while.

- Try to be as friendly as possible to everyone at school, even if you feel shy, and spend time with friends who accept you for who you are.

- Get regular exercise.

- Learn to relax through deep breathing or music or whatever works for you.

- Be hopeful. Many children lose their TS when they get older and maybe one day some clever researchers will learn how to cure it altogether.

## Don'ts

- Don't blame yourself. It's not your fault.

- Don't blame your parents. It's not their fault or anyone else's.

- Don't put up with teasing or bullying. Tell your parents or a teacher who you trust.

- Don't think you're the only one; there are lots of other interesting people who have TS."

"This is my list of do's and don'ts if you don't have TS and you want to help people who do have it.

## Do's

- Try to understand that we don't do our tics on purpose, even if that seems hard to believe.

- Remember we have the same feelings as you do.

- Be friendly and kind.

- You can ask about our tics when you really want to understand but please do it in a kind and friendly way.

- Try to imagine what it would be like to have tics.

## Don'ts

- Don't copy our tics.

- Don't keep on about the tics too much.

- Don't tease or use bad names."

# Facts about Tourette Syndrome

- Tourette Syndrome is named after Georges Gilles de la Tourette, a French doctor who published an account of nine patients with TS in 1885.

- The exact cause of TS is unknown, though many genes seem to be involved.

- Tics involve a disorder in the planning loop of the brain. This is the same loop involved in obsessive-compulsive disorder (OCD)/anxiety.

- There are between 200,000 and 350,000 people with TS in the UK.

- Words that come out in vocal tics are not the person's thoughts.

- TS can lead to trouble with unaware teachers, policemen, bus drivers, etc.

- For TS to be diagnosed by a doctor, both movement and vocal tics need to be present for a minimum of 12 months.

- Treatments include medication, habit reversal training, relaxation techniques such as meditation, yoga and exercise. There is less agreement about benefit from homeopathy, acupuncture or diet adjustment.

- TS affects one in 100 schoolchildren.

- TS does not affect IQ, although learning can be hindered.

- TS occurs three to four times more often in boys than girls. (I have chosen to use "he" and "himself" rather than "she" and "herself" because more boys than girls suffer from TS, but of course these points apply equally to the girls.)

- Only a small percentage of children have coprolalia (involuntary swearing and rude or racist remarks). When the offensive remarks are tics, they are not the person's thoughts and are not intended to be hurtful.

- Rage may be linked to tic suppression. The teacher should talk through the rage attack with the child afterwards. Could he have let out his feelings in a different way?

- Touching his own or other people's genitals in a compulsive tic can be embarrassing and upsetting for everyone. It may be possible for the child to receive training to touch an object or less personal body part instead.

# How teachers can help

- Don't tell the child to stop ticcing.

- Don't punish children for what they cannot help.

- Offer short breaks in lessons.

- Give extra time. Some things take longer for children with Tourette Syndrome.

- Be aware that tics may make writing difficult.

- The feeling of being different from other children can result in low self-esteem. When possible reward the child with praise.

- Some children suppress their tics at school and tic much more often when they go home.

- Medication for tics may cause sleepiness and lack of energy.

- Give longer time to complete tasks and exams.

- Make sure children with TS are partnered with supportive, understanding and kind "buddies".

- Talk to the child's parents as much as possible.

- Some children may tic more at home so a child with TS may have problems finishing homework.

- Work out the best place for a child with TS to sit. For example, some children with tics prefer to sit at the back of the class so that no one can see their tics. Some children concentrate better with a place at the front.

- Some children benefit from a "fidget" object (like a small toy which they can fiddle with).

# How schools can help

- Apply rules flexibly (this means do not expect everyone to follow every rule. Their problems may not fit in with that rule).

- Provide a private place for time out and for tic release particularly if the tics become overwhelming.

- Let *every* member of staff in contact with the child, not just the form teacher and Special Educational Needs Coordinator (SENCO), know about a child's Tourette Syndrome.

- Schools should have a policy about giving pupils their medication.

- When a child with TS moves to secondary school he may need extra support.

- Individual education plans should take account of a child's TS.

- If the child is being teased provide extra supervision at break and at lunchtime.

- Provide a "link person" who will talk to the child each week and ask about any problems he may have.

- Where appropriate, such as when vocal tics are loud, excuse the child from stressful situations such as a quiet assembly.

# Information for parents and professionals

- Tourette Syndrome is not a psychological condition caused by negative experiences, or bad parenting or by a "naughty streak" in the child. It is a genetic disorder with a wide range of tics in different individuals.

- In addition to coping with his tics, a child may also be coping with siblings and/or parents with linked conditions. And, of course, he may well have one or more of these associated syndromes (known as co-morbidities) himself.

- Recent research with secondary school pupils revealed the children's main concerns: the constant and negative presence of tics, the effort to cope with these, worries about their future and about meeting new people ("everyone thinks I'm weird").

- The children said that school could help with academic difficulties, teasing, concentration problems and social interaction.

- They reported that the top factors making tics worse are: stress, frustration, excitement and boring activities. Factors making ticcing less are: physical activity, being with familiar people, doing activities they enjoy (most children with TS are "hands on learners"), relaxing and having a "fidget object" to fiddle with.

- Some teachers discuss TS with their class and this can be helpful. It needs to be done after consultation with the child and his family. There are guidelines for such presentations (see contact details for Tourettes Action in the Recommended reading, organisations and resources section).

- Many children with TS experience bullying (staring, rude comments, copying of the tics, name calling, exclusion). This is why it is important that other children understand TS. Again parents and teachers have a role to play in ensuring no bullying at school and at home and in helping children with TS to make friends.

- Of course it is sometimes difficult for the hard pressed teacher to distinguish between TS related and non TS related behaviour and to always offer ideal levels of support. However, in general children are happier in schools with good pastoral care systems and sympathetic teachers who listen and believe.

- No TICs (teacher induced confrontations!).

- The child featured in this book is only nine years old and thus has not yet experienced transition to secondary school. However, this move calls for planning and support on the part of parents and teachers. The parents need to select the most sympathetic and appropriate school and to visit the school with the child ahead of the move. They should provide staff with written information about TS and information about their particular child's needs, interests and possible problems. Secondary schools, on their part, should take on this information and planning. They should in any case have a non-bullying ethos, policy and practice and perhaps such things as a buddy scheme. The child will also need a sympathetic adult (a link person) to whom he can turn with any problems that may arise.

# Recommended reading, organisations and resources

## BOOKS
### About Tourette Syndrome

Robertson, M. and Cavanna, A. (2008) *Tourette Syndrome (The Facts)*. Oxford: Oxford University Press.

Kutscher, M.L. (2005) *Kids in the Syndrome Mix of ADHD, LD, Asperger's, Tourette's, Bipolar, and More! The One Stop Guide for Parents, Teachers, and Other Professionals*. London: Jessica Kingsley Publishers.

### Books for teachers (parents and other professionals)

Ball, C. and Box, H. (eds) (2008) *Education Issues and Tourette Syndrome: An Introduction for Parents and Schools*. London: Tourettes Action.

Dornbush, M. and Pruitt, S.K. (2010) *Challenging Kids, Challenged Teachers: Teaching Students with Tourette's, Bipolar Disorder, Executive Dysfunction, OCD, AD/HD and More*. Bethesda: Woodbine House.

Hutchinson, S. (2008) *The Good School Guide to Special Educational Needs 2008*. London: Lucas Publications.

Elliot, M. (1997) *101 Ways to Deal With Bullying: A Guide For Parents*. London: Hodder & Stoughton.

## Books for children and teenagers

Other books in the series "Can I Tell You About..."

Chowdhury, U. and Robertson, M.M. (2006) *Why Do You do That? A Book About Tourette Syndrome for Children and Young People.* London: Jessica Kingsley Publishers.

Buehrens, A. (1990) *Hi I'm Adam: A Child's Book about Tourette Syndrome.* Holzminden: Hope Press.

Thom, J. (2012) *Welcome to Biscuit Land. A Year in the Life of Touretteshero.* London: Souvenir Press.

## ORGANISATIONS

**Tourettes Action**
Tourette Syndrome (UK) Association
Help Desk
Tourettes Action
King's Court
91–93 High Street
Camberley
Surrey
GU15 3RN
Phone: 0300 777 8427 (Monday–Friday 9.00 am–5.00 pm)
Email: help@tourettes-action.org.uk
Website: www.tourettes-action.org.uk

This organisation sponsors local UK support groups and has useful material for schools. It also offers a free information pack which includes a list of consultants who are familiar with TS.

**National Tourette Syndrome Association (TSA)**
A USA based organisation.
Tourette Syndrome Association, Inc.
42–40 Bell Boulevard
Bayside
NY 11361
Website: www.tsa-usa.org

This organisation supports internet membership and has many available printed and DVD resources.

**BeatBullying**
Anti-bullying resources, information, advice and support.
BeatBullying
Units 1–4
4 Belvedere Road
London
SE19 2AT
Phone: 0208 771 3377
Website: www.education.gov.uk

## Special needs

Advice for parents available at www.mumsnet.com

Special Educational Needs Code of Practice available at www.education.gov.uk/aboutdfe/statutory/g00213170/special-educational-needs-code-of-practice

# OTHER RESOURCES

## Stories

Fox Eades, J.M. (2005) *Classroom Tales*. London: Jessica Kingsley Publishers.

Leicester, M. (2007) *Special Stories for Disability Awareness (Stories in which the Child Protagonist has an Impairment)*. London: Jessica Kingsley Publishers.

## Games

Plummer, D.M. (2008) *Anger Management Games for Children*. London: Jessica Kingsley Publishers.

Plummer, D.M. (2008) *Self-Esteem Games for Children*. London: Jessica Kingsley Publishers.

Blank, for your notes

Blank, for your drawings

Made in the USA
San Bernardino, CA
08 August 2020